PETS AND WILD ANIMALS

CAT OR TIGER

BY BRENNA MALONEY

Children's Press®
An imprint of Scholastic Inc.

CAT

TIGER

A special thank-you to the team at the Cincinnati Zoo & Botanical Garden for their expert consultation.

Library of Congress Cataloging-in-Publication Data available

ISBN 978-1-338-89977-1 (library binding) | ISBN 978-1-338-89978-8 (paperback)

10 9 8 7 6 5 4 3 2 1   24 25 26 27 28

Printed in China   62
First edition, 2024

Book design by Kay Petronio

Photos ©: 5 left: Nils Jacobi/Getty Images; 8–9: John M Lund Photography Inc/Getty Images; 15: Clara Manolache/500px/Getty Images; 18–19: Arco/G. Lacz/Imagebroker/Alamy Images; 20 main: Suzanne Marshall/Getty Images; 22 main: Nataba/Getty Images; 23: Brian Sedgbeer/Dreamstime; 30 bottom right: Prashant Sethi/Eyeem/Getty Images. All other photos © Shutterstock.

CONTENTS

MEET THE ANIMALS

Cats and tigers are *very* different animals. Cats are smaller pets that live with people. Tigers are big, wild animals that live in nature.

ADULT HUMAN

CAT

TIGER

Cats and tigers have a few things in common. They are both **felines**. Felines are any member of the cat family. Both animals are also **mammals**. Get ready to discover more about what cats and tigers share and how they are different.

MAINE
COON CAT

SIBERIAN
TIGER

FACT

Tigers are the largest felines in the world.

CAT CLOSE-UP

The average pet cat weighs about 10 pounds (5 kg). Pet cats can be long- or short-haired. Their coat, or fur, can be many colors, including white, black, gray, orange, cream, or brown. The most common coat is called a tabby. Tabby fur is streaked with dark stripes.

AMERICAN SHORTHAIR

FUR THAT MOVES
Tiny muscles attached to hairs help fur stand on end.

BALANCE
Cats have flexible spines and use their tails to balance. This helps them land on all four feet if they fall.

NOW HEAR THIS

A cat has 32 tiny muscles in each ear. A human has only 6 muscles per ear.

ADJUSTABLE EYES

The pupils of a cat look like slits. During the day, their pupils narrow to protect them from bright light. At night, their pupils widen to help them see well in low light.

BY A WHISKER

A cat's whiskers are as sensitive as a human's fingertips.

SNIFF, SNIFF

A cat's sense of smell is 14 times greater than a human's.

CLAWS

Cats' claws curve downward, which means that they can't climb down trees headfirst. Instead, they must back down the trunk.

TIPPY-TOES

Cats walk on their toes.

BENGAL TIGER

SENSE OF SMELL

A tiger's sense of smell is not very strong. They don't rely on it when hunting.

SHARPER VISION

Tigers have large pupils that allow more light into their eyes. This helps tigers see best during mornings and evenings.

TIGER TEETH

A tiger's **canine** tooth can be 3 inches (8 cm) long! That's a little smaller than a Popsicle stick.

WILD WHISKERS

Tigers have whiskers on their faces and bodies that pick up information about their surroundings.

RETRACTABLE CLAWS

A tiger's claws can be pulled inside its paws while it walks. This keeps its claws sharp.

Every tiger has its own **unique** pattern of stripes. Unlike most striped animals, the skin underneath the fur is also striped!

TIGER TAILS

A tiger's tail is about half the length of its body.

A tiger can weigh 220 to 660 pounds (100 to 300 kg). Tigers have orange fur with black stripes. Their bellies and the insides of their legs are white with black stripes.

LEAPING LIMBS

A tiger's back legs are longer than its front legs. This helps it leap up to 33 feet (10 m).

Most cats are tidy and spend a lot of time grooming themselves.

FACT

COZY AT HOME

Cats can be found on every continent except Antarctica. Some pet cats live only indoors. Others spend part of their time outside and part of their time inside. Indoor cats like to find cozy places to curl up and sleep.

IN THE WILD

Tigers can be found throughout Asia. They live in many kinds of natural **habitats**. Tigers live in rain forests, grasslands, savannas, and even swamps. Their stripes help them blend in with their surroundings. They stay hidden while hunting **prey**. Tigers seek out water and are very good swimmers.

FACT A tiger's toes are partially **webbed**, which makes swimming easier.

HOME ALONE

Pet cats usually enjoy the company of other cats. Especially if they were raised together from kittenhood. Adult cats can be upset if things change. Introducing a new pet into a home might cause stress to some older cats.

A group of cats is called a clowder, a clutter, or a glaring.

FACT

Adult tigers live alone. They roam across large areas called ranges. A range can be big or small depending on whether there is enough food or not.

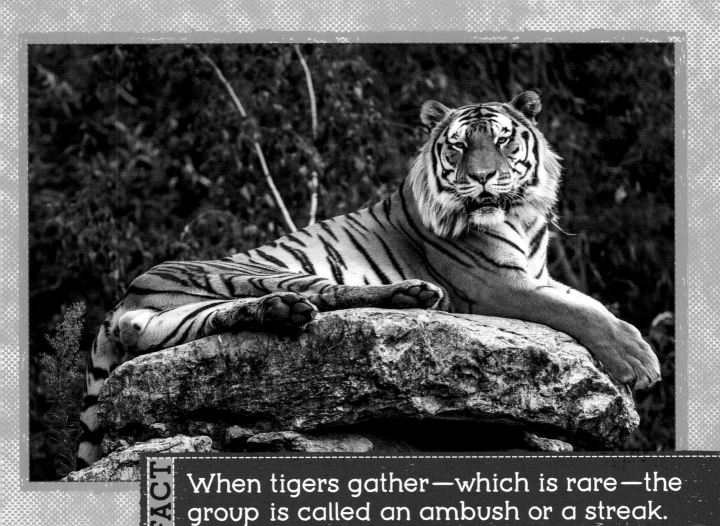

FACT
When tigers gather—which is rare—the group is called an ambush or a streak.

A cat's taste buds can't sense anything sweet. **FACT**

CAT KIBBLE

Pet cats eat meat. Outdoor cats might hunt animals like birds, mice, or other small mammals. Indoor cats are usually fed dry cat food or wet cat food. These foods are made from meat, chicken, fish, and some grains and vegetables. Indoor cats have their food served to them in a bowl.

DINING OUT

Tigers are **carnivores**. That means they eat meat. Their favorite foods are large, hoofed mammals. Depending on where they live, they eat antelope, deer, wild boar, and buffalo. They also eat leopards, crocodiles, wolves, and rabbits. Tigers often sneak up behind their prey to attack them.

In one sitting, a tiger might eat
up to 88 pounds (40 kg) of meat!

CHATTY CATS

Cats can't roar like tigers, but they do purr. They do this when they are happy or relaxed. When cats want to talk to people, they "meow." Meows tell people how a cat is feeling. When cats want to speak to other cats, they trill, yowl, howl, snarl, growl, and hiss.

FACT Cats can make at least 21 different sounds.

Tigers roar. This is a way of speaking with other tigers over long distances. Tigers also grunt, growl, moan, snarl, chuff, and hiss. Tigers cannot purr.

You can hear a tiger's roar 1.9 miles (3 km) away!

TAIL TALK

Cats and tigers "speak" in other ways, too. If a cat's tail is puffed up, and the hairs are standing on end, that cat is feeling scared. It might be trying to make itself look bigger to tell others to stay away.

A pet cat can hold its tail in an upright position while walking.

FACT

Tigers use their tails to talk to one another. A tiger is relaxed if its tail is loosely hanging. Watch out if its tail is moving quickly side to side! That tiger might be mad.

Newborn kittens weigh
about as much as a lemon.

FACT

KITTENS

Mother cats can have **kittens** from spring to late autumn. They can have between four and six kittens per litter. Kittens are small, blind, and helpless. For the first two months, they need their mothers for everything. They grow quickly and are adult size by the time they are 12 months old.

TIGER CUBS

A **tigress** can give birth to as many as six **cubs**. She raises them on her own. Male tigers live apart from their families. Young tigers stay with their mother for two to three years. During that time, she teaches them how to hunt and take care of themselves.

FACT A tiger cub weighs about as much as a cantaloupe when it is born.

NIGHTY NIGHT

Pet cats usually sleep between 12 and 18 hours a day. Cats sleep lightly and wake up often. That's where the term "cat nap" comes from.

Scientists think that both cats and tigers dream when they sleep.

Tigers can sleep up to 20 hours a day. When they are awake, hunting prey takes a lot of energy. When they aren't hunting, they like to rest on their sides in cool, shaded places.

YOU DECIDE!

Now you know what makes cats and tigers so different! If you had to choose, would you rather be a pet cat or a tiger? If you want to be a small cat that lives with people, you may choose to be a pet cat. If you want to be a big cat with a loud roar, you might prefer being a tiger.

GLOSSARY

canine (KAY-nine) one of the pointed teeth on each side of a mammal's upper and lower jaws

carnivore (KAHR-nuh-vor) — an animal that eats meat

cub (kuhb) — a young animal, such as a tiger, lion, wolf, or bear

feline (FEE-line) — any animal of the cat family

habitat (HAB-i-tat) — the place where an animal or plant is usually found

kitten (KIT-uhn) — a young cat

mammal (MAM-uhl) — a warm-blooded animal that has hair or fur and usually gives birth to live babies

prey (pray) — an animal that is hunted by another animal for food

pupil (PYOO-puhl) — the round, black center of the eye that lets light enter

tigress (TYE-gruhs) — a female tiger

unique (yoo-NEEK) — being the only one of its kind

webbed (webd) — having toes that are connected by a web or fold of skin

INDEX

ABOUT THE AUTHOR

Brenna Maloney is the author of many books. She lives and works in Washington, DC, with her husband, two sons, one dog, two pet cats, but no tigers. If she had to choose, she would definitely be a tiger.